Plant Life Cycles

Anita Ganeri

Heinemann

80 002 695 541

Sch

Young Explorer

www.heinemann.co.uk/library
Visit our website to find out more information about **Heinemann Library** books.

To order:
☎ Phone 44 (0) 1865 888066
▤ Send a fax to 44 (0) 1865 314091
▢ Visit the Heinemann Bookshop at www.heinemann.co.uk/library to browse our
catalogue and order online.

Editorial: Jilly Attwood, Kate Bellamy
Design: Jo Hinton-Malivoire
Picture research: Kay Altwegg, Ruth Blair
Production: Séverine Ribierre

Originated by Dot Gradations Ltd
Printed and bound in China by South China Printing
Company

ISBN 0 431 11407 2 (hardback)
ISBN 978 0 431 11407 1 (hardback)
09 08 07 06 05
10 9 8 7 6 5 4 3 2 1

ISBN 0 431 11413 7 (paperback)
ISBN 978 0 431 11413 2 (paperback)
10 09 08 07
10 9 8 7 6 5 4 3 2

British Library Cataloguing in Publication Data
Ganeri, Anita
Plant Life Cycles – (Nature's Patterns)
571.8'2
A full catalogue record for this book is available from
the British Library.

Acknowledgements
The Publishers would like to thank the following for
permission to reproduce photographs: Corbis pp. **4**,
21; Cumulus pp. **8**, **30**; Cumulus pp. **10**, **12** (Holt
Studios International), **28** (Holt Studios International/
Nigel Cattlin); Getty p. **20**; Harcourt pp. **11**, **24**;
NHPA pp. **17** (George Bernard), **7**, **26** (Ernie Janes),
6 (Dr. Eckart Pott), **25** (James Warwick); OSF p. **15**;
OSF p. **29** (Terry Heathcote); Photodisc pp. **5**, **14**,
16, **18**, **19**, **22**, **23**, **27**.

Cover photograph of a dandelion bud, flower and
seedhead is reproduced with permission of Alamy.

Our thanks to David Lewin for his assistance in the
preparation of this book.

Every effort has been made to contact copyright
holders of any material reproduced in this book. Any
omissions will be rectified in subsequent printings if
notice is given to the Publishers.

The paper used to print this book comes from
sustainable resources.

Contents

Words appearing in the text in bold, **like this**, are explained in the Glossary.

 Find out more about Nature's Patterns at www.heinemannexplore.co.uk

Nature's patterns

Nature is always changing. Many of the changes that happen follow a **pattern**. This means that they happen over and over again.

Life cycles are patterns.

Plants make seeds, which grow into new plants. Then the life cycle pattern begins again.

Plant life cycles follow a pattern. A **seed** grows, makes more seeds and finally dies. Then the new seeds grow and make their own seeds. The cycle starts again.

New plants

There are many different kinds of plants. But most of them grow in the same way. Most new plants have a life cycle that starts with a **seed**.

Seeds are made inside flowers. This tree has white flowers.

Conkers are a kind of seed. They grow into huge horse chestnut trees.

New plants **sprout** from seeds. Some plants grow very quickly. Other plants grow slowly. Trees are plants that can take many years to grow to their full size.

Growing seeds

Most **seeds** grow in soil.
They start to grow into plants
under the soil. A seed starting to
grow is called **germination**.

shoot

seed

root

First, the hard case around the seed breaks open. Then a root grows down into the soil. A first shoot grows up and the plant's first leaves begin to open.

first leaves

A seed needs lots of water and sunlight to make it grow.

Rambling roots

A plant's roots grow at the bottom of its **stem**. They are usually hidden under the soil. The roots hold the plant in place so that it does not blow over.

Some plants have fine, thread-like roots.

Trees have huge roots. You can see part of their roots above the ground.

As the roots grow, they get longer and spread out through the soil. There are tiny hairs at the end of each root. These hairs soak up water and **nutrients** from the soil.

Leaves and food

Plants need food to live and grow. We have to find food to eat but plants can make their own. Plants make their food in their leaves. This is called **photosynthesis**.

Plant leaves open to face the Sun. Plants use sunlight to make their food.

The plant's leaves collect sunlight. They use it to mix **gas** from the air, with water from the soil. Inside the leaves, the gas and water are turned into sugary food for the plant.

sunlight energy

A plant makes food from sunlight and water.

water taken up by roots

13

Strong stems

A plant's leaves are fixed to its **stem**. Some stems grow tall and strong. Other stems grow along the ground or curl around other plants for support.

The stem holds the plant's leaves up to the sunlight.

stem

There are lots of tiny tubes inside the stem. Some tubes carry water from the roots to the leaves. Other tubes carry food from the leaves all around the plant.

Some stems grow very thick. They make the trunks of trees.

Blooming Flowers

Some plants grow flowers at the end of their **stems**. Other plants have flowers all along their stems. Flowers make **seeds** that grow into plants.

Many trees and plants grow their flowers in the spring.

bud

A rose flower grows from a rose bud.

A flower grows from a **bud**. Most buds are small and green. They burst open to show their flowers. Many plants flower in the spring and summer.

Inside a flower

There are many different parts inside a flower. These parts make the plant's **seeds**. One part of the flower makes a powdery dust called **pollen**.

petal

pollen

Bees pick up pollen on their bodies and carry it to another flower.

Pollen travels from one flower to another. It joins with part of the new flower to make a seed. Sometimes the wind blows the pollen. Sometimes birds or insects carry it.

19

Sprouting seeds

A **seed** starts to grow inside the flower. Now that the flower has made a seed, its job is finished. Its petals **droop** and fall off, and the flower dies.

This rose has made its seeds. Now it droops and dies.

Inside the seed are the parts that will grow into a new plant. The seed also has a store of food that the new plant can use to grow.

There are lots of different parts inside a seed.

fruit and nuts

Some kinds of **seeds** grow inside hard cases. When you crack open the hard shell of a walnut, you can see the seed inside. This seed is a nut you can eat.

The seed inside is a walnut. It is covered in a hard shell.

The pips inside an apple are its seeds.

Some kinds of seeds grow inside juicy fruits, like plums, cherries and apples. Other seeds, like peas and beans, grow inside cases called pods.

Scattering seeds

The **seeds** need a good place to grow. Some seeds are so light that they blow away in the wind. Other seeds have tiny hooks for sticking to animals' fur.

Dandelion seeds are so light the wind can blow them away.

When birds eat tasty berries, they also eat the seeds inside them. The seeds go through the birds' bodies. Then they fall to the ground in the birds' **droppings**.

If seeds in the birds' droppings land in good soil they start to grow and the life cycle *pattern* begins again.

Growing from bulbs

Some plants die in winter. All that is left of them are **bulbs** under the ground. A bulb is a ball of thick, fleshy leaves with roots and a short **stem**.

Onions are a kind of bulb.

In spring, tulip flowers grow from tulip bulbs.

In spring, bulbs **sprout** into new plants. The new plant uses the store of food inside the bulb to grow. Next winter, the plants die down again.

Dying down

Some plants, like sunflowers, only grow one lot of flowers and make one set of **seeds**. They flower in spring or summer. Then they die in autumn or winter.

These sunflowers only live for a year, then they die.

Some trees can live for hundreds of years.

Some plants, like trees, can live for many years. Each year, they grow new flowers and make new seeds. Some die down in winter but **sprout** again in spring.

How to grow a sunflower

1 Fill a pot with soil.
2 Make a hole, push the sunflower **seed** in, and cover it with soil.
3 Put your plant in a sunny place and water it often.

  Find out more about Nature's Patterns at <u>www.heinemannexplore.co.uk</u>

Glossary

bud the start of a flower or leaf

bulb a ball of thick, fleshy leaves with roots and a short stem

droop go soft

droppings solid waste from an animal

gas air-like material that is not solid or liquid

germinate when a seed grows into a plant

nutrients food living things need to grow

pattern something that happens over and over again

photosynthesis how green plants make food from gas, water and sunlight

pollen powdery dust in a flower

seed contains the parts of a new plant

sprout when a new plant starts to grow

stem a plant's stalk or a tree's trunk

More books to read

Cycles in Nature: Plant life, Theresa Greenaway (Hodder Wayland, 2000)

Life Cycle of a Sunflower, Angela Royston (Heinemann Library, 1998)

Living Things: Life Cycles, Anita Ganeri (Heinemann Library, 2001)

Index